The Collection

a poetic exploration of friendship, love, fantasies, and the soulmate

Jacqueline Belle

Title: The Collection: a poetic exploration of friendship, love, fantasies, and the soulmate / Jacqueline Belle.
Names: Belle, Jacqueline, author.
Description: Poems
ISBN: 978-1-990605-02-4 (softcover) Third Edition

First Edition 2019, ISBN: 978-1-65-234812-2
Second Edition 2020, ISBN: 978-8-74-227369-1

Cover design by Jacqueline Belle on Canva.
Image: It's Her by Jacqueline Belle
© 2024 Jacqueline Belle Poems

JBP Publishing, imprint of Jacqueline Belle Poems
jacquelinebellepoems.com

DEDICATION

To all those that supported and helped me along this
journey and to those that continued to believe in me:
my art, my ideas and my ability.

Jacqueline Belle

There are old stories
that live inside my mind
so familiar
quietly whispered
so many times

I sense the warmth
as my breath flows out
into the space around me

my body, suspended
floating heavy and limp
air pulled from my lungs

I know the end
shall we go back
start again?

Jacqueline Belle
The Collection Revisited

MY MORNING COFFEE

My morning coffee

warms my hands.

Steam curls upward,

creeping slowly,

under my chin.

I breathe in the thick

musky smell

of my mourning brew.

I close my eyes

and enjoy the silence

of the moment.

HE IS HERE

She had been waiting for this moment. She wore her best cotton dress, conservative and comfortable. Thoughts churned inside her head. The possibilities. How would it feel?

Today it was hot. It sat heavy in her chest; thick and humid. A bead of sweat rolled down her spine, dampening her dress. She stepped up to the entrance of the building and breathed in the dense air; gasping slightly. She tugged on the handle of the door and it creaked stiffly as it shifted opened.

One foot stepped and then the other. The door swung shut behind her, bumping her and pushing her slightly forward, further into the corridor. Rushing her. The air changed as she moved inward. A hint of cool swirled around her. Her feet felt like lead; heavy and thick.

She stopped abruptly as the hallway opened into the pub. The room was crowded, every seat taken. People were leaning against every wall, table and chair. The air thickened, the smell of bodies, beer and grease filled her senses. Memories flooded forward; her stomach tightened. She bit her lip gently, turned slightly to the left and began to search the room. Flitting from face to face, scanning the crowd. Laughter, drinking, eating, talking. Dark, light, tall, small, thick and thin. None of them were right. Just not right. Where? Where is he?

The ache in her abdomen tightened, pulling deep, growing.

The lump in her throat was gently choking her; welling up. She bit her lip and swallowed. She pushed down the rising doubt.

The smell of stale beer, sweet apple, sweat and linseed oil permeated her skin. Maybe he didn't come.

She scanned the crowd again, each face unknown. Bouncing from one face to the next. She didn't know what she was looking for. An image created in her mind. It may not match what's real.

Doubt grew steadily, festering, gnawing. Too

old, too young. She'll know him. She'll know when it's him. She knows him from the inside out; she will know.

She bit her lip again, tucked in her chin and breathed deeply. Then she exhaled with firmly rooted feet. Memories bubbling upward, frothing like sea foam, lifting, lifting, changing, laughter and kindness. She lifted her chin, inhaling, eyebrows raised. He's here... but where?

Her eyes darted from face to face; searching. The noise was deafening, pushing against her. Music, yelling, laughter then...

silence...

Suddenly all sound was muffled, edges were blurred; their eyes meet. Time shifts and slows, distorts then with a tiny inhale, joy and a smile burst from within. He stands, a little too quickly, knocking the table, spilling his beer. She doesn't notice. She doesn't care. She isn't here for the drink.

Her heavy feet become light as feathers. She's

barely touching the floor. She glides forward.

Arms, legs, chairs and tables... all part before her. She doesn't notice the bumps, the hands, the calls, *how about a drink lassie?* She hears none of this. Their eyes remain locked.

She flits forward like a moth gravitating toward the light. All else is darkened and fogged over around her. She moves closer, hands outreached. In a moment, their fingertips touch. His hands slide into hers. Joy floods through them. He pulls her forward by the small of her back, their arms wrap around each other, pulling each other closer. She whispers to him. *You are... you feel just as I thought you would feel.* He rests his cheek against her forehead. *You are... you feel sincere my friend.* Her palm reaches up to his temple, hovering just for a moment then sliding down his cheekbone, jaw, chin, neck and resting on his chest. *You are... you feel rough, my friend.* A chuckle bubbles up and out of her. He tightens his embrace and exhales deeply. She can feel the warmth of his breath; his smell is strong, kind and comfortable. She whispers. *You feel just as I thought you would feel. You are... you are my friend.*

Yes, you are, you are my friend... and I am grateful.

Jacqueline Belle

I KNOW

I lean on the rail
        looking out at sea.

The air is fresh, cool, salty.
            I can taste it on my lips.

The wind brushes my hair
            from my cheeks.

It is strong but I feel calm.

I feel you.
I can feel you looking at me.

If I turn, I know you will look away.
        grossly intrigued by the waves,
        the sand, the ship on the horizon.

I've memorized them.
            I know them all.

I know that you know none of them.

I feel you...
        Why don't you let me see?

Jacqueline Belle

I MUST TELL YOU

It is hard,
        but I will.

You may not want to know,
        but you must.

It might hurt.
        Yes, it may.

Will you hold my hand?
        Yes, place it here.
        I am ready.

This,
        this is what I must tell you.

        Okay. It's okay.

UNSAID

Her fingertips rest on his forehead.

Tracing down to his temple.

It gently shifts with her touch.

Fingers curl around his ear.

It is a gentle sensation.

Barely there; breaths are released.

She moistens her lips and continues

      the movement along the jawline.

Using the side of her finger to draw

      her hand closer to his chin.

He swallows,

afraid to move,

anticipation?

She gently places her finger across both lips.

Shhhhh...

REACH UP

There is a world that exists;

    it hovers over each of us.

This is where our dreams live,

    our imagination, our fantasies.

Our dreamland.

As you walk through life,

    reach out to your dreamland.

Reach up and allow your dreams

    to lap at your fingertips.

Allow your imagination to heighten your
senses.

Let reality's sounds, smells, flavours

    and textures to surround you.

Engulf you.

Allow your fantasies to creep up

    and tap you on the shoulder.

Whispering...

    Remember me?

Feel the heat intensify as you pull

    these two worlds together.

Edges form in your dreams.

Your imagination ignites

    and your fantasies play out.

Walk through life; don't run.

Experience the intensity,

    as your passions rise;

    taste fulfillment.

Jacqueline Belle

SNAKE CHARMER

Her cheekbones glisten in the sun.

Eyes steady.

Patient.

She watches without movement.

Barely breathing.

Waiting.

A breeze brushes against her face.

She senses something.

It's nearly time.

Her eyebrow raises ever so slightly.

Her fingertips gently grip the metal.

She watches.

She watches for just the right moment.

Her gaze never wanders.

Her mind is sharp.

He lays coiled

Coiled up, resting.

Resting just ahead.

He knows she is there,

but he cannot look away.

Their eyes lock.

His skin prickles with anticipation.

Gently her body begins to undulate.

Her arms lift gracefully.

It is a dangerous dance.

They both know it.

She parts her lips.

Releases the air from her lungs.

Ahhh... the dance begins.

SOUL SEARCHING

Lay back rest your head.

I`m going to look inside;

    deep inside.

Open your eyes.

Look at me.

Don't look away.

Stay still. Stay very, very still.

I hover above you,

    no body moves.

It's all inside.

Every twitch, every flinch

    can be felt.

Don't move, don't look away.

I'm going in

    deep, deep inside you.

I push away all the filth.

I push aside the murk

    until...

        until I see, a glow.

Don't move.

Don't look away.

Hold my gaze.

I see,

I see inside you.

It glows,

    orange and warm.

I can't hold it...

       just a little longer.

Don't look away. Don't move.

there...

It's hard to breathe.

My heart is racing.

Sweat trickles down my back.

Don't move. Stay very, very still.

I'm almost there.

I can almost... touch it.

In a sudden rush.

All of your memories come forward.

The wind whips my face.

Thrashes my hair.

It's a rush.

Too many, too fast.

Don't move.

Don't look away.

I see them.

I see them all.

I see everything.

HIGH WIRE

It's a strange place,

    between.

This space, this space between,

    seems limitless,

    like an elongated rift.

When you arrive, you can still see

    your dreams floating above

    and

    reality firmly planted below.

You can see,

    you can see both sides.

This space appears endless, expansive.

Yet still just a place, a place between.

To venture into this space,

       is like stepping out onto a high wire.

Feet desperately gripping,

       curling around the wire.

The cold metal cutting into

       the soles of your feet.

Stepping outward...

Arms spread wide

       into the vast space surrounding.

Allowing your fingertips

       to graze the underbelly of your dreams,

       your fantasies.

Pinching the folds,

       pulling them down toward you.

Your body quivers at this touch.

Electricity burns from the tips of your fingers

    down your arms to your body,

    your soul.

But the risk is always present.

    but a breeze,

    or a tremor.

All of which can betray you.

Slipping from the high wire.

Plunging downward.

Passing through the rift

    into reality.

What will become of you?

What will become of you when you fall?

BLINDED

It tickles me gently,

    to watch,

    to watch,

    your stroll, your walk, your path.

I see you trying to cross.

    I see your struggle.

I can see it change,

    I see your mind corrupt.

Your struggles,

    the path, the path is dark.

It can no longer be seen.

I feel your pain,

    your desperation.

I'm trying to reach out,

    for an arm, a hand, anything.

I keep missing,

    I can't...

    it feels frantic.

Our arms are flailing,

    it hurts and our panic rising.

Then,

one hand grabs hold,

    each palm grips the other.

Your body is still,

    hanging limply from my arm.

Hanging over the abyss,

    the endless void between.

The grip is tight.

    The grip is tight.

Jacqueline Belle

IN THE DARK

It was dark and the air was thick.

It sat heavy in my lungs and

        my breath was shallow.

I strained to see.

I could hear you, feel you.

I could smell you,

        but I could not place you.

My pupils held wide as I scanned

        the room around me.

It was then that your presence,

        your location became known.

I could feel the warmth of your body

        behind my right shoulder.

I turned and struggled to see you.

Your heavy breath whispered in my ear.

I froze, waited and listened.

With a sharp inhale,

      I swiveled toward your sound;

      astonished.

It was your words. I heard them.

Are you sure? I asked.

I felt you nod in reply.

But... you know... I breathed.

You know... my voice trembled.

You know that once I release a poem into the world,

      I can't take it back.

My skin prickled

      and my hair stood gently on end.

Are you sure?

Are you sure that you are ready?

The sensation spread throughout my body;

cold and alert.

I acknowledged the answer.

Drew in my breath.

Held it just for a moment.

Then a flurry of letters

and a torrent of words,

language filled the space.

It filled with my thoughts, my words

and my fantasies.

Shapes became elongated,

    the world began to spin;

    everything was a blur.

Time stretched and contracted

    with each breath.

I could feel the world around me

    dissolve and solidify

    almost simultaneously.

The world felt blacker than black.

My feet were firmly rooted into the ground.

My breath slowed.

I lifted my chin,

    searching for a sign of you.

I reached out, groping the air.

I stepped forward.,

      my foot bumped something large.

I knelt down, reached out my hand

      and found you.

You were cold;

      warmth passed down my arm

      through my fingertips to your body.

My hand slid upward to your head.

I touched the hairs on the back of your neck.

Warmth flowed through my hands

      to your skin as I placed them

      on the sides of your jaw.

I turned your face towards me,

    I could see the light behind your eyes.

I warned you...

I warned you this could happen...

Your mouth opened

    and I could feel your cold breath.

I leaned closer,

    bringing my ear to your lips.

I listened. I listened a long, long time.

I placed my hand on your chest and

    allowed the heat to move into your body.

Slowly warming you as you spoke,

    so softly.

When your words stopped,

    I slid my hand behind your back

    and helped you to sit up.

We sat hugging our knees,

    resting our shoulders

    against each other.

The sides of our heads tilted together,

    our breath slowed,

    our eyes closed.

Time stretched as we sat and

    savoured the calm of the moment.

breathe...

Jacqueline Belle

MY TURN

It is my turn to lay awake.

Pondering the web within my mind.

There are so many connections, signals.

Touching, crossing, overlapping.

Confusion leaves me

      Trying...

Trying to understand.

Trying to untangle the web.

To find the path forward.

It is my turn to lay awake.

Jacqueline Belle

BALANCE

Sometimes when I look through

    the magnify glass;

I expect to see the world so clearly.

Each detail, every edge, fine lines.

Instead, I see too much or not enough.

Sometimes when I look through

    the telescope;

I expect to find answers, new worlds,

    something profound.

See each star, every planet, fine particles.

Instead, I see vastness, emptiness, confusion.

How to find balance?

Not falling too deep or lifting too high.

Staying somewhere in between.

Present, calm and in balance.

Jacqueline Belle

NO MORE TUGGING

I stand on the edge,

arms wide,

chin lifted to the sun.

Toes curl

over the edge

of the abyss.

Heels are firmly rooted,

palms raised,

leaning forward.

There is a pull,

upward and back,

tugging.

Jacqueline Belle

The sun shines

down on my skin.

Tug, tug, tug.

The wind blows toward me.

Allowing me

to lean further... reaching.

Ever further...

Toes gripping the edge.

Tugging, tugging, tug.

A warm hand firm on my shoulder.

I turn

and look into your eyes.

I willingly fold inward,

allowing the embrace.

No more tugging.

Just resting in this place.

Jacqueline Belle

THE TREE

There once was a boy; almost a man.

He wore one sock up, left the other one down.

He roamed the land, looking for something.

Searching, searching for the unknown.

One day, he came across a seedling,

    it nearly reached his chin.

He was curious about this small tree and

    decided to stay and watch it grow.

The boy spoke to it softly, when he was lonely.

Watered it and checked on it each day.

He watched it grow and thrive.

The tree grew tall, buds formed.

Its leaves unfurled;

    thrusting open.

Its branches stretched

    reaching upward to the sun.

Soon blossoms formed;

    the petals burst open,

    exposing full colour and beauty.

The tree was grand.

The scent of the blossoms drew others near.

They gathered around the tree.

The beauty of the flowers filled them with joy.

The boy was entranced by the fruit

    forming within the blossoms.

It grew and the branches heaved

    with the weight of the fruit.

He gazed upward, mouth hanging open.

Craving to touch the fruit.

To taste it... just one piece he thought,

    then he would be satisfied.

He gently tugged at the fruit.

Sunk his teeth into the flesh.

Allowing the juices to roll back on his tongue

    and flow slowly down his throat.

He savoured it;

     he felt satisfied.

The boy sat back

     and enjoyed the scene around him.

Day by day more gathered.

They came to smell the fruit

     and enjoy the beauty of the tree.

Some picked the fruit

     and sat with the tree while they ate.

Others looked on from afar.

The boy watched.

He picked more fruit.

Each time he bit into the fruit,

     he craved more.

When he wasn't devouring the fruit,

      he was dreaming of it.

The taste, the smell, the idea of its flesh.

He gathered the fruit as often as he could;

      it was ripe and it was delicious.

The boy filled his pockets, his satchel,

      anywhere he could stash the fruit.

He waddled away; arms laden.

The boy wanted to be alone with his fruit.

Away from the crowds;

      so he could gorge on it in silence.

The boy stuffed his face with the flesh.

Pushing it into his mouth.

Juice poured down his throat, his chin

     and onto his chest.

It stained his skin, his shirt and his trousers.

He filled himself greedily;

     alone.

There was no one to interrupt his gluttony.

The boy slumped in the corner.

Surrounded by the pits of his labour.

Fat; past satisfied.

It made him ill;

    too much, too fast.

The boy lay in his filth.

He sat and digested;

    closing his ears to all sound.

Meanwhile, the tree was in trouble.

A storm came through.

It tore at the branches.

Ripping leaf and stem from its hold.

The tree slumped; branches broken.

The boy lay in his corner, digesting his feast.

He had no need for the tree,

    no hunger for its fruit.

He had all that he desired.

The boy grew healthy

      and began to thrive from fruits energy.

He sat all alone with his thoughts...

      inspired.

The tree called out to the boy;

      calling for help.

Branches broken; the tree moaned in pain.

The ripe fruit lay rotting

      around the base of the tree.

The tree slumped, branches dragging.

The boy did not come;

      he did not want to hear.

He was busy in his thoughts.

But there were some that did.

They heard the tree's cries.

There were some that noticed.

They gathered slowly around the tree.

Humming and caressing the tree's bark.

Mending its branches; watering the roots.

The fallen fruit added nutrients to the soil.

The tree stood tall; new leaves uncurled.

Many stayed with the tree

      or waved as they passed by,

The tree was filled with joy

      but longed for the boy and his visits.

The tree thrived all the same;

      stretching, growing, surviving.

The tree grew taller; wiser.

Its bark thickened

      layer upon layer of memories.

The bark hardened

      and the branches lifted high into the sky.

Now the tree bears no fruit within reach,

      these branches are tainted

      and lay bare.

No longer can one come to freely pick the fruit.

On occasion, the tree may choose

      to gently drop its fruit.

But only to those who will savour the scent,

      the sweetness of the nectar,

      slowly and thoughtfully.

Do you savour? Are you thoughtful?

Do you nurture and respect your tree?

or do you arrive at harvest,

    licking your lips; fork in hand?

Who do you choose to be?

MY HEART LAYS OPEN

My heart lays open

to those I share.

Tiny scratches,

lesions...

My heart lays open

to those I trust.

Bruises,

scars form.

My heart lays open

open to all.

How long?

How long will it last?

How long,

Before,

before I am numb?

Jacqueline Belle

SUBTLE SADNESS

There is a

subtle sadness

in the ability

to remember

fine details

over long periods

of time...

SOMETIMES

Sometimes

when everything

around you

is bleak

full of sadness

and despair

all you need

is your friend

to sit down

beside you

talk about nothing

laugh at everything

roll around on the grass

until your cheeks

and sides ache

sometimes

this is all

one needs.

Jacqueline Belle

COME TOGETHER

When joy and sadness brush hands...

we find something...

we find it when the prints of fingers

rub gently against each other.

The minute sensation,

it is the faintest tickle

that radiates along the finger and hand,

up the arm, through our shoulders

and into our chests.

This is where it stays and rests awhile.

If we listen closely,

we will find it.

We will find

humility

and grace.

Jacqueline Belle

SETTING SUN

The setting sun

warms your body,

your mind.

Allows

regeneration

from within.

Reach out

and gather

the strands of hope

from all around you.

Clutch them close

to your heart,

and never let them go.

Jacqueline Belle

PURE AND SIMPLE

Pure and simple

nothing more, nothing less.

The hollowness

and emptiness

of the heart yearns

to be filled.

Not with

the harsh reality

of lust

but tenderness

and acceptance

that softly turns

with a gentle step

into the sunlight.

Pure and simple

Nothing more, nothing less.

CHERISH

Your voice calls out.

I wait, unwavering.

I hear your whispers.

Sitting back on my heels.

I listen without judgement.

Feeling sweet peace and tranquility.

I hear the sound of your voice

Your words are chewed, tasted,

savoured and digested.

They radiate deep inside my body.

Your voice bursts forward,

without hesitation

or trepidation.

In times of joy, my palm is flat.

Our arms are lifted towards the sun.

The enjoyment, the happiness.

rushes through our bodies as one.

In times of darkness,

I curl my arms around you,

empowering, shielding.

Simply protecting.

In times of joy,

my little feet dance,

I reach up to your finger.

I allow you to guide and lead our dance.

The feeling of love spreads

with each step.

In times of darkness,

I stand firm footed; arms outreached.

Creating a protective ring of fire around you.

Providing strength, courage and support.

We place our hands together.

We forgive.

The feeling grows and strengthens

within our chests.

Pushing outward, there is no stopping.

No one can touch us now.

A look of the eye.

Fire burns, yearning grows.

Our gaze locks, raw desire ignites.

The passion is exhilarating,

consuming.

The dance moves forward,

quickening, slowing,

never dying.

We lean inward, foreheads together;

we breathe.

This... this is what it means to be cherished.

BUT A MOMENT

We walk hand in hand

       along the shore.

Our toes dig into the sand

       with each step we take.

Waves crash;

       the breeze whispers to us.

Caressing our shoulders

       urging us onward.

You lift your arm

       bringing mine with it.

I dip under and

       my skirt swirls as I move.

Our smiles grow.

We look off into the distance.

It is but a moment,

    a moment in time.

Jacqueline Belle

TRUST

I offer you my hand.

I wait patiently, calmly,

    firmly outreaching.

I wait.

        I peek over the side of your hand.

          Tentatively, I climb your

            curled fingers.

           Slowly cautiously.

I hold steady, firm.

Take your time.

There is no rush.

Time stands still.

My tiny fingers are clinging to the

grooves and crevasses

of your hand.

Each path is unique.

My hands are gradually morphing,

from the efforts of my labour.

I watch you traverse the

changing landscape.

I slowly nudge closer.

Closer to the centre of your palm.

I am cradled by the calluses

and folds of your skin.

I feel your touch.

It's calm, graceful, yet powerful.

I feel you as your body curls up in my palm,

resting warm and safe.

Held in the palm of your hand.

Free, yet secure.

I create a sense of belonging,

peace and tranquility.

The longer I stay,

the stronger the feeling becomes.

IT IS STILL DARK ...

It is still dark,

    the sun has yet to rise.

My eyes begin to open slowly,

    blinking.

My breath is slow,

    My eyelids are heavy.

A yawn creeps upward.

As I release it,

    My body stretches ever so slightly.

I turn,

    I can feel the crisp cotton

    brush against my skin.

In the darkness,

        I can just make out your profile.

Your eyes are closed,

        your mouth slightly open.

I trace your lips with my eyes.

I can hear you breathing.

It...

        it gives me a smile.

I nuzzle closer

        resting my head on your shoulder.

I close my eyes

        and go back to sleep.

Jacqueline Belle

LOVE CAN BE...

Love can be...

gentle and subtle;

    dry leaves rolling slowly

        along the ground in the breeze.

or ferocious and rough;

    a tooth baring deer in rut.

Love can be...

sad and melancholic

    a feather brushing past

        your temple and sliding

            down to your chin.

or full of laughter and joy

    as humour bursts forth

        and your body succumbs,

allowing it to bubble

and froth upward;

releasing into the world.

Love can be...

painful

a pain that hurts so delightfully good

a passionate squeeze

or a fire that burns so deeply within...

it can only be experienced

with mutual surrender... ecstasy.

or silent

a silence that takes up

so much space

there is no room for anything else.

Love cannot be...

it cannot exist, in any form,

    without a mutual foundation...

a foundation of trust, honesty, respect,

    loyalty and acceptance.

Love requires this solid base...

    from both sides,

    something strong to build upon...

    or it will collapse

        like a house of cards.

SATISFACTION

My foot touches the ground,

a stick snaps,

leaves crunch,

the soil compresses under my weight.

A gentle breeze,

caresses my skin.

Pushes the silk of my dress

against my legs.

My hair brushes from my face.

I hear the rustle of leaves.

The bare trees surrounding me

have no shadows.

I lift my arms

    reaching up to the moon above.

I can feel myself lifting,

    so gently.

The tops of my feet lap at the forest floor.

Ever so slightly,

    tickling the tips of my toes.

My lips part,

    stretching back slowly into a smile.

My eyelids relax

    and drift into closure.

The sound of the wind

flows over me.

Lifting me higher,

lifting me... softly.

The sound, so intricate, so complex

yet so simple.

I'm lifted forward

and higher into the sky.

I can feel the glow of the moon on my face.

Warm and refreshing.

The silk of my dress caresses my skin;

goosebumps rise.

Every sensation amplified.

I reach and stretch my arms further

my hands extended.

I pass through a layer of cloud

cleansing my skin,

my sorrow,

my fear.

Washing it all away.

Above the cloud, my body settles

moving slowly and gently

along the river of mist.

My body undulates

with the rise and fall

of each ripple.

I float along the river

      with, with the sound of the wind.

I let my arms relax.

Allowing my fingertips to caress the vapour.

The touch is so lovely, so pure.

Love spreads up through my fingers,

      my arms and into my body.

Resting in my heart,

      elevating my soul.

Warmth radiates from my body.

Peace and tranquility.

I am content.

As I reach this moment of peace and bliss,

      the wind begins to slow.

I feel myself sink

    through the river of cloud,

    into the open space below.

Satisfaction grows as I descend.

I slip through the bare trees

    and slowly to the ground.

The breeze sets me down

    with gracefulness

    upon the forest floor.

Silk as my blanket.

Moss as my pillow.

I drift into slumber

    so deep.

Comfort surrounds me.

EPILOGUE - GO FORTH

Self,

do not go where I went before.

Move forward

on the path unknown.

See

what I have not seen.

Feel

what I yearn to touch.

Go forth.

Do not dwell here with me.

The future lies ahead.

Jacqueline Belle

NOTE:

The Collection: a poetic exploration of friendship, love, fantasies and the soulmate was originally published in 2019. The third edition, published in 2024, has replaced two poems *Sadness* and *Hope*. These two poems are published in Belle's first poetry collection, *When I Walk Upon the Earth*. To avoid repetition, the decision was made to replace them with the poems: *Sometimes* and *Setting Sun*. Two additional poems were added to the third edition, *Subtle Sadness* and *Pure and Simple*. I hope you enjoy your journey with *The Collection* revisited.

ABOUT THE AUTHOR

Jacqueline Belle is a poet, author, creator,
and voice artist. Jacqueline has three published poetry
collections: *When I Walk Upon the Earth*, *The Collection:
a poetic exploration of friendship, love, fantasies, and the
soulmate* and *The Weight of the Universe*. Jacqueline has
lived and travelled throughout the world. Her stories and
poetry reflect the people she has met and the places she
has seen along the way. To learn more about her
creations, visit:

https://JacquelineBellePoems.com
https://JBellePoems.carrd.co